Tiger Sharks

Samantha Bell

Published in the United States of America by Cherry Lake Publishing
Ann Arbor, Michigan
www.cherrylakepublishing.com

Consultants: Dominique A. Didier, PhD, Associate Professor, Department of Biology, Millersville
University; Marla Conn, ReadAbility, Inc.
Editorial direction: Red Line Editorial
Book design and illustration: Sleeping Bear Press

Photo Credits: iStockphoto/Thinkstock, cover, 1, 11, 13, 19, 21, 25, 27, 28; A Cotton Photo/Shutterstock
Images, 5, 9; Sleeping Bear Press, 7; Dorling Kindersley RF/Thinkstock, 15; Amanda Cotton/iStockphoto,
17; Greg Amptman's Undersea Discoveries/Shutterstock Images, 23

Library of Congress Cataloging-in-Publication Data
  Bell, Samantha.
  Tiger sharks / Samantha Bell.
      p. cm. — (Exploring our oceans)
  Audience: 008.
  Audience: Grades 4 to 6.
  Includes index.
  ISBN 978-1-62431-410-0 (hardcover) — ISBN 978-1-62431-486-5 (pbk.) — ISBN 978-1-62431-448-3 (pdf)
  — ISBN 978-1-62431-524-4 (ebook)
  1. Tiger shark—Juvenile literature. I. Title.

  QL638.95.C3B45 2014
  597.3'4—dc23   2013006184

Cherry Lake Publishing would like to acknowledge the work of
The Partnership for 21st Century Skills. Please visit www.p21.org
for more information.

Printed in the United States of America
Corporate Graphics Inc.
July 2013
CLFA11

ABOUT THE AUTHOR

Samantha Bell is a children's book writer, illustrator, teacher, and mom of four busy kids. Her
articles, short stories, and poems have been published online and in print. She loves the outdoors,
nature, and animals, but she will not be going into the ocean at dusk anymore.

TABLE OF CONTENTS

CHAPTER 1

A FIERCE PREDATOR

When people think of sharks, they usually think of great white sharks. But the tiger shark is also one to watch out for. With its huge jaws and sharp teeth, this "trash can of the sea" eats whatever it can find. Tiger sharks mostly catch other marine animals. But tiger sharks have eaten man-made objects too. Tiger sharks have made meals of boat cushions, coiled wire, coal, nuts and bolts, and canned food. They are also known for attacking people. It's a good idea to stay out of this shark's way!

Tiger sharks are strong ocean predators.

Tiger sharks are found around the world. They swim in all tropical and subtropical waters, except for the Mediterranean Sea. They are one of the most common sharks in the Caribbean Sea and the Gulf of Mexico. Tiger sharks can be found near the coasts of North Carolina, South Carolina, Georgia, and Florida. Swimmers and surfers in Hawaii are also on the lookout for them. Most shark attacks in Hawaii are from tiger sharks.

Many tiger sharks don't stay in one place. Some **migrate** when the seasons change. They move from the tropics to more **temperate** water during the summer. Then they go back to the tropics in the winter. Tiger sharks have been seen as far north as Great Britain in the Atlantic Ocean. They have been spotted as far south as Australia in the Pacific Ocean. Their migration could be 1,000 miles (1,609 km) or more. Scientists tagged one tiger shark that spent the summer near New York and the winter near Costa Rica—1,800 miles (2,897 km) away. They can travel about 10 miles (16 km) in a day.

THINK ABOUT IT

THINK ABOUT OTHER ANIMALS THAT MIGRATE. WHY DO THEY MIGRATE? ARE THESE REASONS SIMILAR TO OR DIFFERENT FROM THE REASONS TIGER SHARKS MIGRATE?

RANGE MAP

Tiger sharks live mostly near continents.

Tiger sharks are found in the open ocean and near the coasts. Adults spend a lot of their time just beyond the edge of a reef. They can also be found in deep water over a **continental shelf**. They can dive down to depths of about 1,085 feet (331 m). They swim to the surface to eat. Tiger sharks go where food is, which also means the murky waters along a shore. They can be found in harbors, lagoons, and even in the salty water at the mouth of a river. These areas attract a lot of animals. They also attract tiger sharks that want to eat the other animals.

Tiger sharks are some of the most-feared sharks. They rank number two in attacks on humans, just behind the great white. People need to be cautious around these extremely dangerous animals. However, the remarkable creatures can still be appreciated. ◢

Researchers continue to study tiger sharks in order to learn more about the species.

CHAPTER 2

STRIPES AND MORE

Tiger sharks, especially juveniles, are easy to recognize. They are bluish-green to dark gray on top and off-white below. Like tigers, they have stripes and spots along their backs and sides. These markings are darker in younger sharks. The markings fade as the sharks get older. Sometimes they disappear altogether.

Tiger sharks are some of the biggest sharks in the ocean. They have long slender bodies. They have large heads with wide mouths and blunt noses. An adult tiger shark can range from 10 to 14 feet (3.0–4.3 m) long and

Tiger sharks are easily recognized by their spots and stripes.

LOOK AGAIN

LOOK AT THE STRIPES ON THE SHARK.
DO YOU THINK IT IS YOUNGER OR OLDER?

weigh from 850 to 1,400 pounds (386–636 kg). One of the largest tiger sharks recorded was 17 feet (5.2 m) long and weighed about 2,000 pounds (907 kg). That's almost as much as a small car!

Like all sharks, the tiger shark does not have bones. Instead, its skeleton is made of lightweight **cartilage**. This helps it "hover" in the water. The tiger shark also has a large liver filled with oil. The oil weighs less than water. This also helps keep the shark afloat. The shark's pectoral fins and tail provide lift too.

Both male and female tiger sharks have thick skin that helps protect them. Shark skin feels smooth when stroked from front to back. When it is stroked the other way, it feels very rough. Tiny tooth-like scales called **dermal denticles** cover the shark. These create a sort of armor. They also reduce the drag a shark has as it swims through the water. This allows the shark to move more quickly.

A white belly helps a tiger shark blend in with lighter waters above it. This helps the shark sneak up on prey.

Sharks do not use their noses for breathing. Sharks are fish, so they use their gills to get oxygen. When water enters the shark's mouth, it passes over the gills. The gills take the oxygen from the water. The water then moves out through the gill slits. Tiger sharks have special gill slits right behind their eyes. These provide oxygen directly to the eyes and brain.

The fierce reputation of the tiger shark comes from its bite. Like other sharks, they have several rows of teeth. When a tooth is lost, it is quickly replaced by one behind it. Tiger shark teeth have a unique shape. One side of a tooth has a large curve. It is similar to the blade of a can opener. A smaller curved edge is behind it. All of the edges are extremely sharp. The teeth are **serrated** like the blade of a saw. This design works well for the tiger shark. First, it bites into the tough skin or shell of its prey using the bigger side of the tooth. Then it tears into the food using the smaller part.

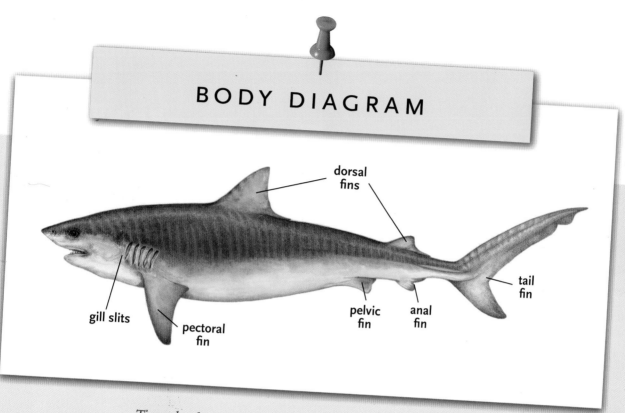

BODY DIAGRAM

dorsal
fins

tail
fin

gill slits

pectoral
fin

pelvic
fin

anal
fin

Tiger sharks are some of the largest sharks in the ocean.

Tiger sharks can eat prey that is almost as large as they are. They have elastic muscles and hinged joints in their jaws. This allows them to open their mouths very wide. Records show a 12-foot (3.7 m) tiger shark once ate a 10-foot (3.0 m) shark. ◢

Eating Anything

The tiger shark lives up to its name when it prowls the ocean waters. It hunts alone after dusk. The tiger shark searches for its prey just below the surface of the water.

Tiger sharks have good night vision. They also use other sensory organs to find food. Hearing is one of their longest-range senses. Sharks have inner ears inside their heads. The inner ears pick up sounds coming through tiny holes on top of the head, just behind the eyes.

Tiger sharks can hear sounds from hundreds of yards away. Tiger sharks are mostly attracted to fast or irregular sounds. These sounds might be made by a struggling or injured animal.

Tiger sharks have the ability to open their mouths very wide.

In moving water, a shark can detect the smell of blood hundreds of yards away. It can also figure out the direction that smell is coming from. The shark swings its head from side to side as it swims. It gathers the smell in its nostrils. One nostril will sense the smell more strongly. The shark will turn and move in that direction. It continues to follow the trail as the scent gets stronger and it finds its prey.

As with all sharks, tiger sharks also have a lateral line system along both sides of the body. These special organs detect vibrations in the ocean. Animals moving through the water create vibrations. The sharks can sense where the animals are by using these organs.

All living things produce electrical fields. Even the smallest movement of a muscle creates an electrical field. This electricity doesn't travel through air. Yet it travels well through water. Sharks have special organs called ampullae of Lorenzini. These look like tiny holes around a shark's nose and mouth. The organs detect electricity. The shark can use its ampullae to find prey. But motors also create electrical fields. Sometimes sharks mistake them for food. A biologist studying seals once saw a tiger shark attack and eat his boat propeller.

A tiger shark's strong sense of smell helps the shark find prey.

LOOK AGAIN

LOOK CLOSELY AT THIS PHOTOGRAPH. WHAT FEATURES DO YOU SEE THAT HELP THE SHARK HUNT AND EAT?

Tiger sharks eat almost anything that floats. When a tiger shark picks up the scent or vibration of a large animal near the surface, it will investigate. Younger, smaller sharks eat mostly fish and birds near or on the surface. Larger sharks go after bigger prey such as dolphins, seals, and sea lions. Stingrays and other sharks are also on the menu. Common meals include crabs, conches, jellyfish, and sea snakes.

Tiger sharks are known to migrate between island groups. They do this to take advantage of the food supply. At certain times of the year, colonies of young birds learn to fly over the water. Tiger sharks are there to eat the birds if they fly close to the water or land on the surface. At the Great Barrier Reef, the sharks migrate at the same time green sea turtles are nesting. The sharp teeth of a tiger shark can break a turtle's hard shell in half.

Tiger sharks have also been known to eat manmade objects. These include empty cans, small barrels, and a roll of tarpaper. Even explosives have been found in a tiger shark's stomach. Items that can't be digested will sit in a shark's stomach for a while. Later the sharks will throw up these man-made objects. It is no wonder the tiger shark is considered one of the most adaptable shark species. ◢

Tiger sharks have strong jaws that crush their prey.

CHAPTER 4

PUPS AND GROWING UP

Depending on where they live, tiger sharks **mate** either in the spring or fall. In the Northern Hemisphere, they mate from March to May. In the Southern Hemisphere, mating season is from October to December. Pregnancy lasts for about 14 to 16 months.

Once a tiger shark is pregnant, the eggs develop and hatch inside the mother. Each baby shark has its own yolk sac. This supplies the shark with nutrition as it grows. The baby shark also receives a kind of creamy milk from the mother.

The **pups** are born from April to June of the next year in the north and from November to January in the south. The mother gives birth to anywhere from 10 to 80 pups. The young are gray or grayish-brown with spots or stripes. They measure 20 to 30 inches (51–76 cm) long.

A tiger shark pregnancy lasts more than a year.

While adult tiger sharks are fearsome and powerful, tiger shark pups are not. Newborn tiger sharks are slender and delicate with oversized fins. Their tails aren't much help, as the sharks can only wriggle through the water. Predators are everywhere. The pups are often in danger of being eaten by crocodiles, seals, and larger sharks. Since they can't move quickly, their best defense is to hide. Because tiger sharks have so many pups at one time, at least some of the pups will be able to escape.

The pups and juvenile sharks often remain close to the shallow area where they were born for some time. Those that survive grow quickly. The pups usually double their length within the first year. The sharks are full-grown after four to six years. Males reach a length of 7 to 9 feet (2.1–2.7 m). Females are between 8 to 10 feet (2.4–3.0 m) long. The sharks are then ready to mate, and more pups will be born a year later. Once grown, the tiger shark has few enemies and can live to be about 12 years old. ◢

Tiger sharks' stripes can help them blend in to their surroundings.

LOOK AGAIN

LOOK CLOSELY AT THIS PHOTOGRAPH. WHERE COULD A TIGER SHARK PUP USE ITS STRIPES TO HIDE FROM PREDATORS?

CHAPTER 5

THREATS

Tiger sharks are **apex** predators. They are at the top of the food chain. The size of an adult tiger shark is enough to protect it from other animals. It is too big for most other predators to try to eat it.

The main threat to tiger sharks comes from humans. Both **fisheries** and individuals try to catch them. Fisheries can sell many of a tiger shark's parts. People use tiger shark skin to make leather and the liver to make vitamin oil. The fins are used to make shark fin soup.

The fishing industry may have a negative impact on the tiger shark population.

Sportfishermen go after the sharks as a game fish. Fishing regulations are in place, but they are hard to enforce.

GO DEEPER

WHAT IS THE MAIN IDEA OF THE PREVIOUS PARAGRAPH? PICK OUT EVIDENCE THAT SUPPORTS THIS IDEA.

If a tiger shark attacks someone, people become frightened. A big shark that comes to a tourist beach endangers the visitors. It can also ruin the businesses of the people who work at the beach. One way authorities have tried to prevent more attacks is by killing all the tiger sharks in an area.

But killing the sharks can lead to more problems. Sharks help keep the **ecosystem** in balance. For example, animals such as sea turtles eat among the sea grass beds. Without the tiger sharks to keep the turtle population down, the sea grass beds would disappear. An important **habitat** would be lost.

Tiger sharks keep the sea turtle population down, which helps keep sea grass ecosystems balanced.

People also try to limit shark attacks by making barriers to keep them out of swimming areas. Nets are often used, but the sharks sometimes get caught in them and die. Other barriers have been tried. These include walls of bubbles, underwater sounds, watchtowers, shark fences, and small electrical fields. Unfortunately, these are often very expensive to keep up.

One of the best things people can do to avoid shark attacks is to understand the sharks. Often, the number of attacks in an area has more to do with the way people behave than the way sharks behave. Swimming in areas where sea turtles and other marine animals are found invites a shark attack. Playing in murky water can confuse a shark. It might mistake an arm or a leg for a small animal. Fishing boats close to shore may throw blood and bits of fish into the water. This attracts sharks. Ships that throw their leftover food overboard lead the sharks right into the harbors.

Predicting shark behavior isn't easy. All sharks behave differently. People need to be careful around them, but these sharks have a place in the ocean. ◢

THINK ABOUT IT

▲ Think about what you knew about sharks before reading this book. How are tiger sharks similar to and different from what you thought?

▲ In Chapter 3 you learned how a tiger shark finds its prey. If there was an injured pelican floating on the water, which of its senses do you think the shark would use to find it? Why?

▲ Who do you think is more dangerous, tiger sharks or people? Why?

▲ If all tiger sharks were gone, there would likely be fewer shark attacks. What else might be affected?

LEARN MORE

FURTHER READING

MacQuitty, Miranda. *Shark*. New York: DK, 2011.

Marsico, Katie. *Sharks*. New York: Scholastic, 2011.

Musgrave, Ruth. *Everything Sharks: All the Facts, Photos, and Fun That You Can Sink Your Teeth Into*. Washington, DC: National Geographic Society, 2011.

Parker, Steve. *100 Facts on Sharks*. Thaxted, UK: Miles Kelly, 2010.

WEB SITES

Discovery Kids—Sharks
http://kids.discovery.com/gaming/shark-week

This Web site lets readers learn about shark attack survivals and play games.

National Geographic—Sharks
http://animals.nationalgeographic.com/animals/sharks

Readers discover different species of sharks, learn more about the ocean, and play games at this Web site.

GLOSSARY

apex (AY-pex) at the very top

cartilage (KAHR-tuh-lij) a hard, flexible tissue that forms certain parts of animals' bodies, such as a human ear or a shark's skeleton

continental shelf (kahn-tuh-NEN-tuhl SHELF) the part of the sea floor that slopes into the water before a steep drop to the ocean floor

dermal denticle (DUR-mul DEN-ti-kuhl) a sharp, tooth-like piece, such as the scale of a shark

ecosystem (EE-koh-sis-tuhm) the interaction of organisms and their environment

fishery (FISH-ur-ee) the industry of catching, processing, and selling fish

habitat (HAB-i-tat) the place where an animal or plant usually lives

mate (MATE) to join together to produce babies

migrate (MYE-grate) to move from one area to another

pup (PUP) a baby shark

serrated (SER-ay-tid) looking like the blade of a saw

temperate (TEM-pur-it) not extremely hot or cold

INDEX

[21ST CENTURY SKILLS LIBRARY]